DINOSAUR
Discovery

Brown Watson
ENGLAND

STRANGE CREATURES FROM THE SEA

The Earth's first creatures lived in water. Some of them are shown here. The largest animal alive today also lives in the sea. It is the Blue Whale, which is believed to be the largest creature that has ever lived. It can grow to over 33 metres in length, and weigh around 190,000 kilos.

NOTHOSAURUS (NOT-o-SAWR-us)
200 million years ago

This long-necked, long-tailed reptile was a great fish-eater. It grew up to 6 metres in length, had webbed feet, and could move about on land.

DINICHTHYS (die-NICK-this)
200 million years ago

The name of this armour-plated hunter means 'terrible fish'! It grew to a length of 10 metres, and it had an enormous mouth, full of vicious teeth.

PLESIOSAUR (PLEEZ-i-o-SAWR)
150 million years ago

This beast was a descendant of the Nothosaurus. The name means 'swan-lizard', but really they looked more like long-necked turtles. While swimming, they kept their head up out of the water.

BASILOSAURUS (BA-sil-o-SAWR-us)
35 million years ago

An early form of whale, 28 metres long the Basilosaurus looked like a giant sea snake with a mouth containing very sharp teeth.

THE FIRST LAND MONSTERS

Life on Earth began in the sea, where it remained for hundreds of millions of years. The first creatures crawled out of the water to start moving about on land some 300 million years ago.

DIPLOCAULUS (dip-lo-CAWL-us)
280-230 million years ago

Living mainly at the bottom of pools and only occasionally coming onto the land, the Diplocaulus was about 60 cm long. We do not know why it had such a strange, wedge-shaped head.

MASTODONSAURUS
(MAST-o-don-SAWR-us)
270 million years ago

This beast resembled a huge frog, with a head which was over a metre long, bigger than the head of any other amphibian (a creature which lives on land but lays its eggs in water), living or extinct. Its small, weak legs made it awkward on land.

EDAPHOSAURUS
(e-DAF-o-SAWR-us)
270 million years ago

These odd animals had a powerful skull,
and, making use of their crushing teeth,
they probably fed on shellfish from swampy
areas. Their 'sail' helped both to heat and
cool their 3½ metre-long body.

THE 'UNREAL' LIZARDS

When the bones of some of these great dinosaurs were first discovered, people could not believe that such vast creatures ever really lived on Earth. The name Apatosaurus, meaning 'Unreal Lizard', was given to one particular giant.

APATOSAURUS (a-PAT-o-SAWR-us)
150 million years ago

Another name for this plant-eater is Brontosaurus, or 'Thunder Lizard'. 21 metres long, weighing over 30,000 kilos, it must have made a noise like thunder when it moved!

ALLOSAURUS (AL-lo-SAWR-us)
150 million years ago

Although it was less than half the size of a Brontosaurus, this fierce, flesh-eating dinosaur, over 9 metres long, could easily kill the larger, slow-moving, defenceless beasts.

THE LONGEST AND THE LARGEST

Some of the plant-eating dinosaurs grew to a truly enormous size. Much of their lives was spent in lakes, where the water helped to support their weight.

DIPLODOCUS (dip-lo-DOK-us)
150 million years ago

The longest dinosaur measured nearly 30 metres from its head to the tip of its long tail. Like the other giant plant-eaters, it stayed in water for most of the time, out of reach of its fierce enemies.

BRACHIOSAURUS
(BRAK-i-o-SAWR-us)
100 million years ago

This was the largest of all dinosaurs, with front legs that were longer than its back legs. Measuring 12 to 25 metres long and weighing up to 50,000 kilos, with its neck lifted up it would have been able to look straight into the third-storey window of a house!

ARMOURED DINOSAURS

Some of the slower-moving species of dinosaur were only able to survive by developing various kinds of armour. Some of them became like living tanks!

STEGOSAURUS (steg-o-SAWR-us)
140 million years ago

Up to 10 metres long, and sometimes weighing 10,000 kilos, this giant plant-eater had two rows of sharp, bony plates on its back, and a tail armed with four strong spikes.

SCELIDOSAURUS
(SEL-id-o-SAWR-us)
170 million years ago

One of the first of the armoured dinosaurs, the Scelidosaurus was about 3½ metres long, with bony plates all down its back.

THE FIRST FLYING REPTILES

While the giant reptiles ruled the dry land, other species took to the air. They were called Pterosaurs, which means 'wing reptiles'. Their wings were made of sheets of skin, fastened to an extra-long finger on each 'hand', just like the wings on bats today.

DIMORPHODON (die-MORF-o-don)
160 million years ago

This was one of the earliest of the flying reptiles, and its head was very large in comparison to its body. These creatures probably hung upside down from rocky ledges, or tree branches, when they were at rest.

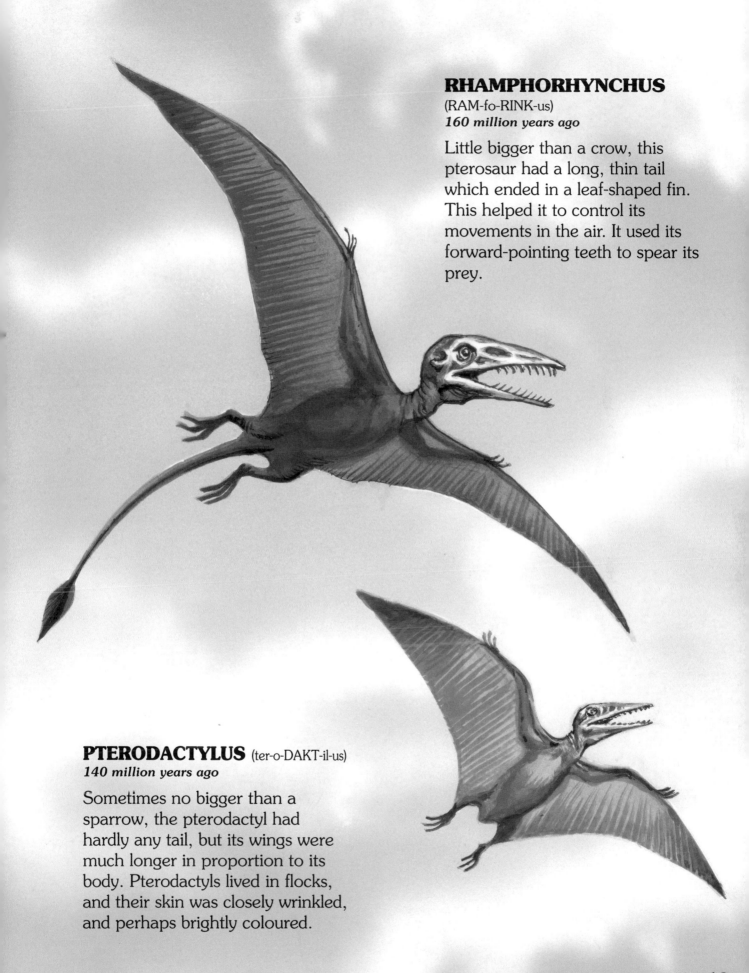

RHAMPHORHYNCHUS
(RAM-fo-RINK-us)
160 million years ago

Little bigger than a crow, this pterosaur had a long, thin tail which ended in a leaf-shaped fin. This helped it to control its movements in the air. It used its forward-pointing teeth to spear its prey.

PTERODACTYLUS (ter-o-DAKT-il-us)
140 million years ago

Sometimes no bigger than a sparrow, the pterodactyl had hardly any tail, but its wings were much longer in proportion to its body. Pterodactyls lived in flocks, and their skin was closely wrinkled, and perhaps brightly coloured.

THE 'HORRIBLE LIZARDS'

Around 80 million years ago, there arose a species of dinosaur called 'deinodonts', which means 'terrible teeth'. They were blood-thirsty predators, who fed on the herds of plant-eating reptiles which lived in the ferny forests and swamps of the time.

GORGOSAURUS (gor-go-SAWR-us)
100 million years ago

Over 3½ metres long, this flesh-eating reptile was a savage beast. Its name means 'horrible lizard', and it was probably very clumsy in its movements. Most likely, its main food consisted of the carcasses of already dead dinosaurs.

TYRANNOSAURUS
(tie-RAN-o-SAWR-us)
80 million years ago

Its name means 'tyrant reptile'.
6 metres in height and over 15
metres long, it was the largest
flesh-eating animal that has ever
lived on land. Its front legs were so
short they could not even reach its
mouth, and it carried its long tail
upright as it moved, in order to
balance the weight of its enormous
body.

THE 'CROOKED LIZARDS'

A new species of dinosaur was descended from the Stegosaurus pictured on pages 10-11. The name given to this species was 'ankylosaur', meaning 'crooked lizard', because of the curved ribs of all these strange creatures.

SCOLOSAURUS (SCOL-o-SAWR-us)
100 million years ago

About 6 metres long, with an armour-plated back, its short legs kept this dinosaur close to the ground. It was only in danger when enemies, like the Gorgosaurus, shown on pages 14-15, were able to turn it over, exposing its unprotected stomach.

ANKYLOSAURUS (an-KILE-o-SAWR-us)
80 million years ago

This was a massive, slow-moving beast, over 7 metres long. Its back was covered with bony plates, which had long spines at the edges. Its head was also armoured, and its tail ended in a heavy, bony club, which could break the leg of a Tyrannosaurus.

THE 'BIRD-FEET' and THE 'DUCK-BILLS'

Two other amazing groups of dinosaurs are the 'ornithopods', meaning the dinosaurs with 'bird feet', and the 'hadrosaurs', which were dinosaurs with beaks like a duck's bill.

IGUANODON (ig-yew-AHN-o-don)
100 million years ago

5½ metres high and 11 metres long, the Iguanodon moved swiftly over the ground on its back legs, with their great three-clawed feet. When attacked, it used its long thumbs like daggers.

CORYTHOSAURUS

(ko-RITH-o-SAWR-us)

100 million years ago

These 'duck-bills' had webbed feet and mouths containing about 1,000 teeth! The one shown here was gigantic, over 12 metres long, with a bony crest like a helmet on its head.

THE 'HORNED FACES'

About 80 million years ago, herds of great four-footed dinosaurs roamed slowly over the plains. They had wide, bony collars round their monstrous heads, which were armed with long horns. They were the 'Ceratops', or 'Horned Faces'.

TRICERATOPS (try-SER-a-tops)
80 million years ago

As the name suggests, this great beast had three horns, two long ones above the eyes, and one on the nose. It was 8 metres long, weighed over 9,000 kilos, and had a huge, hooked beak.

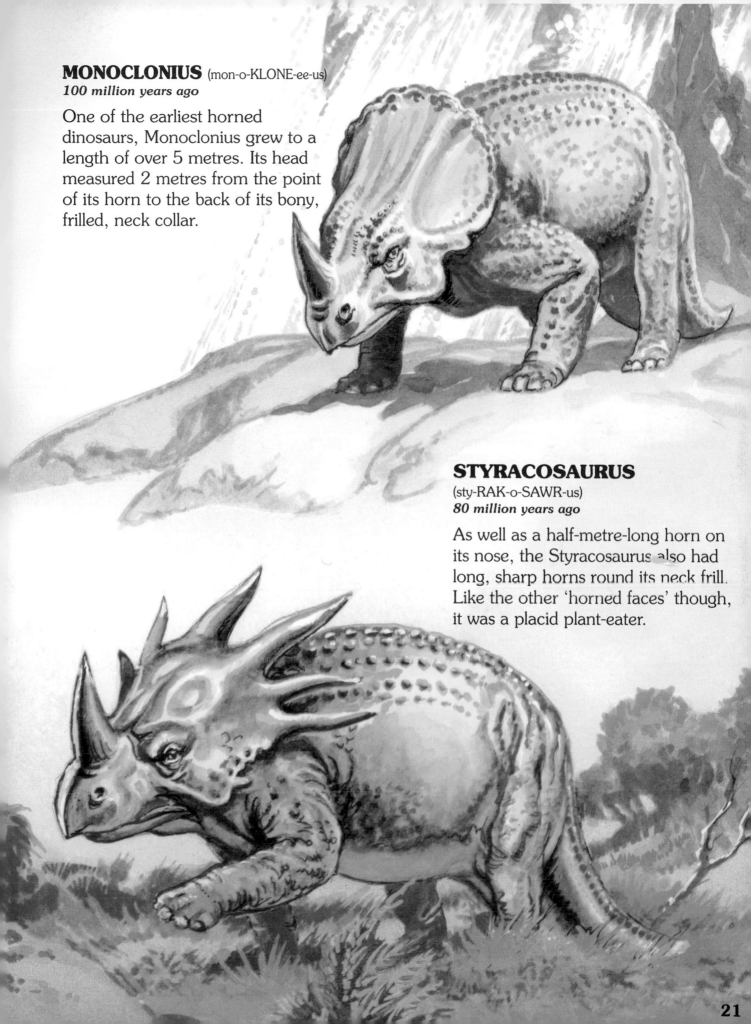

MONOCLONIUS (mon-o-KLONE-ee-us)
100 million years ago

One of the earliest horned dinosaurs, Monoclonius grew to a length of over 5 metres. Its head measured 2 metres from the point of its horn to the back of its bony, frilled, neck collar.

STYRACOSAURUS
(sty-RAK-o-SAWR-us)
80 million years ago

As well as a half-metre-long horn on its nose, the Styracosaurus also had long, sharp horns round its neck frill. Like the other 'horned faces' though, it was a placid plant-eater.

FLYING LIZARD TO FIRST BIRD

100 million years passed from the time of the winged reptiles shown on pages 12-13 to the last appearance in the skies above the Earth of the 'flying dragon' called the Pteranodon, which had a wing-span of over 8 metres.

ARCHAEOPTERYX (ARK-ee-OP-ter-ix)
140 million years ago

This was an extraordinary creature, halfway between a reptile and a bird. It had the teeth of a reptile, the long tail of a lizard, proper hands on the front of its wings, and it was covered in coloured feathers.

PTERANODON (ter-AN-o-don)
60 million years ago

The strange head of this creature extended to the rear in a bony comb. Its long, pointed snout was toothless. It flew by gliding, rather than by flapping its wings, so it must have swooped low over the sea in order to spear the fish that it ate.

THE ORIGINAL SEA SERPENT

Long, long ago, the seas were home for two different types of giant dinosaur. One type, like the Elasmosaurus shown here, had a neck twice as long as its body, and was probably the very first sea serpent. The other type, like the Kronosaurus, had a large, strong head.

ELASMOSAURUS (ee-LAZ-mo-SAWR-us)
100 million years ago

Because of its neck, the Elasmosaurus grew to a total length of 14½ metres. Its paddles, though, were short, so it was not a fast swimmer. It caught fish by swinging its head about swiftly.

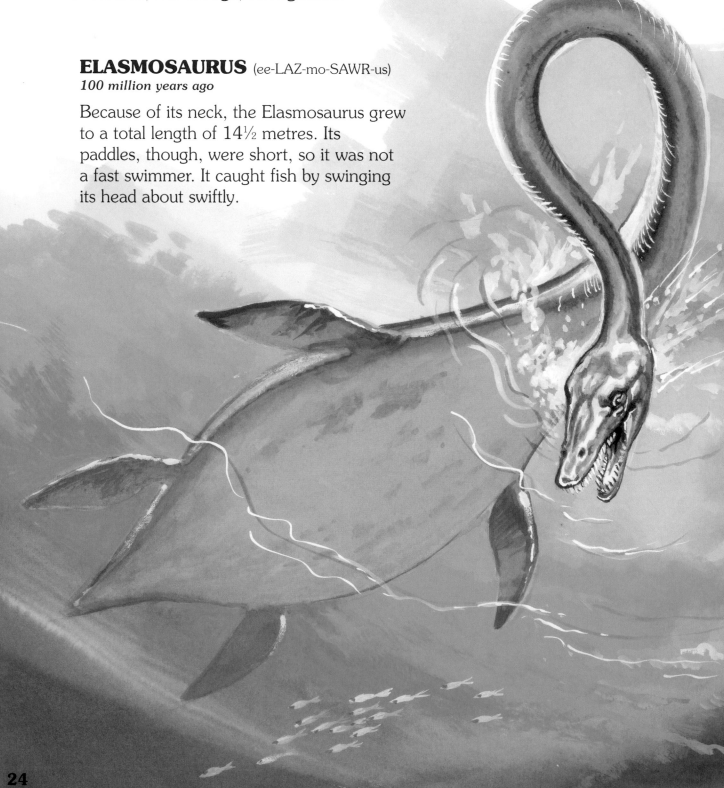

KRONOSAURUS (KRO-no-SAWR-us)
100 million years ago

The head of this frightening beast was over 3 metres long, and it had the biggest mouth of any dinosaur. A man could have passed through it very easily. In appearance, it was like a 13-metre-long crocodile!

'DAWN HORSE' TO 'THUNDER BEAST'

About 60 million years ago, the dinosaurs disappeared. We still do not really understand why this happened so suddenly. After ruling the Earth for 200 million years, their place was taken by mammals, warm-blooded creatures which give birth to living young. Man is a mammal.

EOHIPPUS (ee-o-HIPP-us)
36 million years ago

The first horse is called Eohippus, which means 'Dawn Horse'. It was about the size of a fox, its neck was short, and it stood on tiny hoofs. It was well fitted for survival, as it could run fast, and hide easily in the shadows.

BRONTOTHERIUM
(bron-toe-THEER-ee-um)
25 million years ago

An early relative of today's rhinoceros, the Brontotherium, or 'Thunder Beast', was a clumsy, plant-eating animal, over 4 metres long, with hoofs and horns, and a brain no bigger than an orange.

MEGATHERIUM
(MEG-a-THEER-ee-um)
2 million years ago

Its name means 'Great Beast', and it grew to a length of over 7 metres. Though it was bigger than the largest elephant, the Megatherium could stand on its hind legs in order to eat the leaves in the tree-tops.

GIANT MAMMALS, GIANT BIRD

Some early relatives of animals we know today were gigantic. Shown below are three mammal giants, and one truly remarkable bird.

ALTICAMELUS (AL-tee-ca-MEL-us)
20 million years ago

The camel that crosses our deserts once had a relative that looked like a giraffe! Alticamelus (the name means 'high camel') was 4 metres high, with a long neck for feeding on treetops.

DIATRYMA (DIE-a-TRI-ma)
50 million years ago

In Brazil today, there is a bird called the cariama. It is a type of crane. The Diatryma was an early relative. Though unable to fly, it was a strong runner, with an eagle's beak. It was 2 metres high!

INDRICOTHERIUM
(in-DRIK-o-THEER-*ee*-um)
30 million years ago

Also an early rhinoceros, but even bigger than the Brontotherium on pages 26, this was 5 metres high, one of the largest land animals ever. It had no horns, and lived in small herds, eating leaves.

DINOHYUS (DINE-o-HIE-us)
20 million years ago

Believe it or not, even though the Dinohyus was as big as a large bull, it was a pig! It was nearly 2 metres high, and its back was covered with a bristly mane.

'LEFT-OVERS' FROM THE PAST

Some animals today look much the same as they did in prehistoric times. They have survived for millions and millions of years with very little change.

COELACANTH

This fish dates back to 300 million years ago. Until just over 50 years ago, it was thought to be extinct – like the dinosaurs. Then, one was found off the coast of South Africa, and others have been seen since.

TUATARA

These lizard-like reptiles can be found in New Zealand, and are the only ones left of a group that lived 170 million years ago. The name means 'having spines', as the tuatara has a row of spiny scales all down its back.

TURTLES and TORTOISES

They are the oldest type of living reptiles, and have been on earth for around 175 million years! The proper name for all of them is turtle, but the types that live on land are usually called tortoises.

CROCODILES

Crocodiles and alligators are a group that roamed the world 100 million years ago. They haven't changed much. If you want to know which is which, look at their closed mouths. You can see a crocodile's long teeth, but not an alligator's.

Contents

Index

This edition first published 2006 by
Brown Watson, The Old Mill
76 Fleckney Road
Kibworth Beauchamp
Leicestershire LE8 0HG

ISBN: 0 7097 1756-3

Printed in the E.C.

© 2006 Brown Watson